THE DARING OF PARADISE

ESSENTIAL POETS SERIES 202

Canada Council   Conseil des Arts
for the Arts   du Canada

ONTARIO ARTS COUNCIL
CONSEIL DES ARTS DE L'ONTARIO

50 YEARS OF ONTARIO GOVERNMENT SUPPORT OF THE ARTS
50 ANS DE SOUTIEN DU GOUVERNEMENT DE L'ONTARIO AUX ARTS

Guernica Editions Inc. acknowledges the support of
the Canada Council for the Arts and the Ontario Arts Council.
The Ontario Arts Council is an agency of the Government of Ontario.
We acknowledge the financial support of the Government of Canada through the
National Translation Program for Book Publishing for our translation activities.
We acknowledge the financial support of the Government of Canada through the
Canada Book Fund (CBF) for our publishing activities.

BRIAN DAY

THE DARING OF PARADISE

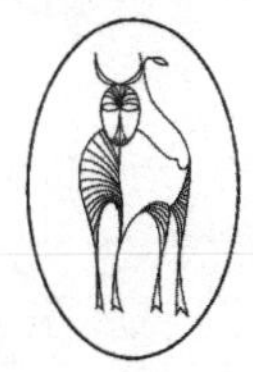

GUERNICA
TORONTO – BUFFALO – LANCASTER (U.K.)
2013

Michael Mirolla, editor
Guernica Editions Inc.
P.O. Box 117, Station P, Toronto (ON), Canada M5S 2S6
2250 Military Road, Tonawanda, N.Y. 14150-6000 U.S.A.

Distributors:
University of Toronto Press Distribution,
5201 Dufferin Street, Toronto (ON), Canada M3H 5T8
Gazelle Book Services, White Cross Mills, High Town, Lancaster LA1 4XS U.K.

First edition.
Printed in Canada.
Legal Deposit – Third Quarter
Library of Congress Catalog Card Number: 2013931300
Library and Archives Canada Cataloguing in Publication
Day, Brian
The daring of paradise / Brian Day.
(Essential poets series ; 202)
Poems.
Also issued in electronic format.
ISBN 978-1-55071-711-2
I. Title. II. Series: Essential poets series ; 202
PS8557.A916D37 2013   C811'.6   C2013-900636-2

CONTENTS

Eyes Turn Blue

With his eager articulate finger, God touches
the first pendant drop of semen and fondles
it calmly in the rainclouds of his mind, turning it

tenderly as he gives face and skin to the formless,
creating the world from the sap of his longing.

The heavenly lover of smoothness and liquids
dangles jewels of water on the bodies of boys,
on their sleek enticing skin of pearl,

and our eyes turn blue with the terror of his beauty.
God lures us with globes of a succulent future,

promising his little ones what he can't grant us
yet, as he toys with the pleasures of grapes
and boys. He invites us to a riverbank

lush with oyster, pearl, and wine,
where our mouths are immaculate organs of knowledge.

We recline on soft couches and are served
luscious fruits, our vision tickled by exquisite boys
rich with sculpture's dark lustre and grin,

boys as comely as virgin pearls.
And our eyes turn blue with the daring of paradise.

Conversion

The universe holds a secret. You could
    call it God, but that may mislead you. You could try
Beloved, Adored, or simply Friend. You might
    use Krishna, Shiva, Buddha. You might call it the light
of the Torah, the breath of the Earth, the lamp
    of all the awakening world. You might,
as the nearest you can reach with the words
    you know, call it Messiah, Anointed One, Christ,
the bright cup drawn up from where there was no well.
    On the day this grateful secret finds you, your
every desire is met by religion's body. You're
    unseated, unmanned, knocked flat to the ground
by its lumens of beauty. Your life is the same –
    it's just that gravity's intentions have changed.
The secret one shines in a circle of beauty
    here at the templed core of your life,
and this beauty now owns your allegiance
    far more than any statable truth.
Arguments, diluted, run through your hands.
    You are in your every tissue a lover, a novice
of folly. You live in that enduring wonder
    when your fiercest desire is revealed
in every crevice of the world. You are whirling, ecstatic,
    wounded by beauty, bereft in a harsh theological
blindness, and aware of the blasphemy to all you had called,
    in your ignorance, God. A brilliance is dictated

line by line here on the thirsting inside
    of your ransomed skin, and you
are a phrase of beauty that can sing of such
    unbounded beauty. You are
in your ancestry plainly human, but now
    you're a severing of air where this secret breathes;
you are this widely flung-open window
    to a beckoning, dear, and dearer world.

Paul, Apostate

He dwells in a secret that can barely
pass his lips, the adoration of a man
that no Jew could entertain. He's the witness
to the secret he's heard whispered
across the gauze of his skin.
The love marks of Jesus
are impressed on his body, and a
gentile devotion is unleashed
in his eyes. What he's tried
to strike down he now knows
to his core: that an image
of man holds the essence of God.
It's love that scours the ancient
teachings from his skin, incites him
to discard those worn patches
of history, to dance as he torches
the scrolls of the Torah. God
has whispered a secret, a sublime
dirty joke, a precious lubricious
new passage of scripture. What Paul sees
in the masculine statue of Jesus,
this one image saved from Sodomic
destruction, is the sudden, unexpected
consummation of his life, his chance to heal
in one image the rift in his world. And the pagan
that was hiding in the heart of God
is revealed at this chosen moment
in time. And Paul is called to be
its apostle, to refashion his life to deal
this bright secret. This will be his repeated

death and resurrection: to die to the bitter
divisions he has known and rise
ridiculed, a scandal, on the further side.

A New Husband

What makes us tick is our lust for the holy.
We lie in bed sleepless, husbands sound beside us,
our skin glowing with the imagined touch of our beloved,
our every thought dancing in the circle of that flame.
For all our married life we've been living in exile,
diverting elsewhere the heat of our ardour.
We have turned ourselves to glass coffins of skin.
It is a death, nearly our own, that buys our freedom.
Now our faded, serviceable lives are behind us,
and our lusts through their long and scriptured repetitions
have worn a traversable path in our hearts.
We glide from funereal rites to the right of new feeling,
through death to that marriage on the further side.
Here, where all adulterous dreams are fulfilled,
prohibition is lifted like a fine bridal veil,
restrictions sliding like silk from our newly formed skin
as our love now progresses from spirit to flesh,
the hands on us rich from each stroke of imagining.
And the one every pore of us hungered for a glance of,
who is the sheeting of our flesh in its wishes,
he is, in all his transfiguring radiance, here.
We step to him fresh from the vestments of death,
lovely with the polish of long nights of desire –
moving from a marriage of decency and contract
to this marriage sweet as the finest adultery.

I Know a Man

I know a man
            who is not me
for no one
            who has known such things
could be a man
            as I am a man.

I know a man who's been lifted in strange levitation,
plucked to that purity of perception
I might call heaven, and shed
beneath him all the sureness
of his flesh. I know a man
whose tongue has been taught the antiphons
of angels, whose organs have been burnished
by seraphic brilliance, the black of whose brain
has been lanced with stars.
I know a man who has held in his nostrils
the perfuming ether of breathable
knowledge, known the ache of it
pounding and singeing his lungs. I know
a man who has heard a crystalline cataract of speech
poured as a thunderous gift to his ears, a man
who has been blinded by words that no
human tongue could hold the storerooms of awe
to repeat. I know a man who has heard inhuman language
igniting all the standing forests of his mind, sweeping up
into blazing what will never be destroyed,
who has heard illicit locutions sung and fluted

through the back alleys of heaven, a man who has known
indecipherable script pressed
as genetics into his memory, whose flesh is now
precious with the trilling and imprint of song.
I know a man who has met before his death
that singular dazzlement of flame
and face, who's been pressed to the maddening
limits of endurance by that vast stunning chorus
when the universe sings in all the octaves of its voice.

I know the exalting and branding
                              wild memory
of a man who was granted
                          some moment of heaven,
a man who was drenched
                        in the depths of God.

Megha

The man who will become the Buddha
    has exchanged all the coins of his begging for flowers –
those blends of pale yielding flesh and light.
    He awaits the arrival of a consummate man
who bears in his skin all the marks of perfection;
    and this man who exudes the scent of nirvana
steps to the street with the steps of a cloud.
    And the man who will become the Buddha
tosses the sumptuous flowers from his hands –
    like cups of light at his own wedding;
and each of the instantly assembled crowd
    adds to the air the delicate petals
that they have plucked from the riot of their lives.
    Flowers ascend – but not one falls,
hovering like flags, like prayers on nothing,
    a temple of cool and rippling fingertips.
They shimmer as a shrine about this man,
    play on the air that envelops his beauty,
form windows and doorways for glimpsing his skin.
    The mind of the man who will be Buddha
dissolves in this reverent moment of beholding,
    and the thousand smooth tongues of the world hold still.
The body of the man who will be Buddha
    yields to his own divine attraction,
steps through the ethereal threshold of flowers
    to fall at the lovely firm feet of this man.
And with the sweeping dark hair of his head
    he strokes these fine bones, these ankles and toes,
absorbed in devotion, sheltered in flowers.
    And the man who feels himself swelling toward Buddha
is now less a human than a curtain of air,
    a trembling of petals where we step between worlds.

Veil of Flesh

We glide through the welcoming veil
of Christ's flesh, through sheerness and panes
of corporeal light, the threshold of the holy
an undulant and yielding brocade of skin.
We move through the thick and blood-dark curtains,
through the many gauzed gates of his one
gracious body. We tread on the crimson path
of his ravishment, part each thin covering
that would shield us from him. He calls us
to step through the rustle and hush
of each sheet of his flesh, and we advance
as invited, through fold upon fold. We enter
through this fine and severing film,
are altered in the very composition
of our cells, as we in antechamber,
chamber, sanctum, become the secret sacred
one he is, home in this wonder that is
his body. We press through light
that gilds our skin as we pass from ourselves
to our radiant selves. We enter
and enter where we are baptized
in bodily knowledge, where we are made
the gleaming initiates of Christ.

Prince of the Universe

We are drawn toward God by the messenger's
beauty, by the trail of fine hair
leading us down the midline
of his torso. We are drawn
by the one we approach with elusive
words but never see incarnate in oils
or stone. He trembles
on the edge of the human precipice,
a hair's breadth from the plunge to fusion
with God. And he is the prince not merely
of men but of all the great grave
constellations, the beloved of the cosmos in all
its dark motions. He is, in his elegant
modesty of beauty, the key
to the piled ripe fruits of paradise, the precision
of his slim fine physique clicking
open that well-oiled lock. We
are called by the calligraphy
of his body's lines, the suras
that are written in his movements
on air. We are bound to him in religious
beauty, bound by the entrancement
of his ambered skin. We share in the secret
passion of our maker for the one whose scent wafts
from the wrists of the world. We are
as besotted, as ruined as God, loving this one
whom God also fervently, shamelessly loves.

Blue Memory

I wanted you born inside me, I wanted
    to recite you, to hold you on my tongue.
    I wanted the codes of your beauty
in my blood. Your words fit
    to each fingered glove of my ear,
        wooed me till I knew no purpose
but you. You gave yourself to me, your seed
    in my belly – the mature and sweetened
        essence of myself. And I grew
as only a boy could, full of you And now
    I am nothing but the temple, the swimming
        blue memory of where you have been.

Luke

a future alive and undarkened
by glass, his face
reconfigures mine as an angel,
and wings issue
like cries from the blades
of my back as he invests
my flesh with this
gravity of light and
whispers the name he's kept
hidden beneath heaven's pillow,
uncovering in me
some unlooked-for beauty, huddling
embered in the thicket
of my skin, and he draws
me up to the surface
of this world
where I breathe in some
foreign, airier element
and expand as the saving
white scent of lilies,
my life at once
a templed bell whose one
struck note cannot dream of
its end, and I am alive
in the gathering of his eyes, in
this vaulting expanse of
wonder and blue, and here
I will always brim
with my own salvation
and live in this body
still angeled with light

You Had Just Stepped Out

You had just stepped out from the party.
You had just stepped out to fetch
a cherished bottle of wine.
And I knew then what men
had held secret for centuries,
that you with the scent of wine
on your breath, you with the merriment
of flavours in your blood, and all that cavorting
glimmer in your eyes – you
were today's visitation of the Friend,
and I could hope for no one
more gracious, more agile, more fitted
to the companionable needs of my soul.

You had just stepped out,
and I was alone with the guests at the party, alone
with my thirst for your particular wine.
And our distance at that moment was
astronomically perfect, my thirst for you sweet
as bright wine in my mouth. And you, in your robust
absence, glowed softly about me like the body
of the moon. You were beautiful, forbidden;
you were absent, imminent, and you were,
without questing or capture, mine.

Religious Puberty

Despite feeling still too young, unformed,
trepidatious of the dizzying ascent to adulthood,
we are, our cravings announce, no longer children,
and what lures us toward a life of religion is no longer
mere mimicry or conscience but lust. The world
has slipped naked into our dreams, and we want
our hands roaming and knowing the whole of that body.
We want to praise it and taste it with the precision
of our lips, the full palate of our mouths. We turn
as if before some forbidden beauty and ask
what this life, this wonder might desire of us. We listen
for the whisper of the world's proclivities,
eager as a trembling novice lover to fulfil the sleek details
of its every request. And sometimes we know,
without a word spoken, what will bring this plenitude
in pleasure to its knees. Our bodies, these newly
invented and now near-insolent instruments of freedom,
have become the creatures that prompt and incite us;
and we, the extravagant graduates of innocence,
propel our prayers with our full bodies' ardour.
We slip within the sheets of carnality's covenant
where the urgencies encoded in a childhood of stories
rise in fresh joy to the flush of our skin.

Jacob, Wrestling

All of his family has crossed over the river
    and Jacob stands for this one night alone.
And out of the mist between dusk and the river
    a man steps unbeckoned with the falling dark.
He is Jacob's perfect match in stature and strength.
    And Jacob gazes on a face all his days have imagined,
a face still obscure when a mere breath away:
    cloaked in its own indefinite majesty
and denying not a letter of Jacob's hopes.
    He suspects an embrace, as from a brother
before the man lunges, aims to thrust him to the ground,
    surges like fire as it leaps toward his tent.
The apparition assaults him with muscle and wings,
    a man torquing swiftly into angel and God.
Jacob takes his place as God's dear contender,
    matching him deftly in this argument of strength.
And God in a gesture of intimate violence
    touches the hollow of Jacob's thigh,
discovering and striking in caress and assault.
    Jacob's partner rips him bone from socket,
unknitting the one knit in his mother's womb.
    Day breaks upon their masculine grappling,
and now by the light in Jacob's eyes
    this entire sweating body shines as God's face.
And the one who challenged Jacob now begs to be let go.
    But Jacob won't release the straining figure in his arms,
demands of it his further birth-right and blessing.

In their nightful of struggle, as they've held to the twist
of sinews and bones, they have wrestled with names,
    the divine and the human writhing in their hands
until the only name they are left with is Striving.
    And Jacob is named Israel, is named Striver with God:
the one who embraces and resists his creator –
    who himself thrills to this defiance of his will.
Israel is left beautifully, limpingly injured,
    his body bruised with the handprints of his maker
and unsteady as clay that refuses to be cast.
    This struggle has torn him to his second birth
and leaves him with this name shining brilliant on his skin.

Law of the Flesh

A coup has occurred within the ramparts
of my flesh, and a new voice directs each deployment
of my will. The body burns, and peace
has passed beyond my understanding,
the law in my parts as imperious and inexorable
as any commandment chiselled in stone.
Not all God's dictates are written on the heart
but inscribed through the whole great book of the body.
Flesh proclaims and insists on
its unalterable law, not caring much for the prancings
of the spirit. And flesh admits no higher
aspiration, nothing less tactile than answering skin.

And would it not be the gravest
betrayal of God to refuse the wild blessings
of this physical life, to scorn this law as innate as breath,
to desecrate the great library of carnal knowledge
and profane the one body God's given to me?
I will not relinquish my hold on religion
until I have bent it to match my own
body's angles, until it has learned the letters
and the verses of human need. I will not
be bullied by a religion written only in my heart.
I will be written all over with the law of God.

Tonguing the Mouths

Though I tongue the mouths of men like angels,
partake in every pharmaceutical rapture, and perform
all pornography's elaborate gymnastics;

though I sculpt with hellenistic precision each limb
of my body, fortify my physique with liquid muscle,
and burn its surface to a mineral hue;

though I test and tune with formidable skill
the pealing cymbals that ring out in my flesh;
though I welcome the nameless hands of adoration

that survey each crafted contour of my form,
and delight in the Babel of tongues on my skin;
though I dance in a body lathed in the workshop of angels

and know my own ecstatic pulse
within the sweet cells of the music's heart;
though the field of my flesh is repeatedly harrowed

and scattered with the seed of seraphic men –
yet if I know heaven only within this heaven
of flesh and find no sweetness in the clearing

where no venturing sense can probe; if I am exalted
by none of the sumptuous cognates of awe;
discern no galleries of radiance beyond

this fine-woven scrim of skin, and part
my lips with no wondering names
for this stunning profusion I'm blessed to receive –

then I am merely a creature of my age;
I am a body unstitched from history,
no more than the handsome simulacrum of a man,

a paragon of polished and unconductive flesh;
I am a mere dabbler in the disciplines of bliss,
not pressing beyond this bright note of elation

to where I am carried line by succeeding line
and I'm swept in a reckless nakedness of spirit,
coursing with the rivers and the tongues of joy.

Pursuing our Pleasure
in the Body of Christ

There is no further body of Christ but this smoothed
     aggregate
of human flesh. We are the athletic limbs
of his swimming through the world, the hands of all
his practical acts. But hands and limbs are not all of a body,
and those parts of Christ we might conceal
must elicit from our mouths a particular esteem.
The body of Christ is built for delight, and not one
of its vivifying organs can be scorned. The kindling sites
of our communal body take part in our sacred
and carnal commission, this ignition of flesh in its
     knowledge
as flesh. We caress the completeness of our one body,
     explore it
with palms, alert it with fists. We lick a glistening
array of physiques, knowing the foreign and knowing
ourselves, knowing Christ in each of his tissues and
     hollows,
straining toward completer knowledge in this keen
     narcissistic
congregation of flesh. We train each finger, each muscle,
     each
follicle to take its place in the communion of Christ.

    And we,
so flooded with desire for the countless strong members
of the body of Christ, what should we in desire
strive for? We would strive to be those zones
of the holy within the common body of Christ, the seats
of pleasure where he excites himself
into vibrant and ever more electric being.

Frog

Religion is seldom a handsome thing.
Grotesquely amphibious, not knowing its place,
it slaps up to your door in its puddle of muck,
stinking of the fetid waters of your past –
that septic stew you had sprinted away from.
It croaks in creation's most unmusical voice,
demanding a payback you'd thought it would not
have the gumption to claim. It squats there throbbing,
a tiny green tyrant, a transmogrification of all you've
ignored. It taunts you with its louche and lurid
innuendos, and its gravelly repetitions leave you pale.
It is the ghost and golem of your playthings:
archaic carnality there on your doorstep.
Who'd have imagined those dwarfish legs, obscene
with muscle, would propel it all the miles to the palace,
that it would pound so loudly on your solid door?
What choice now but to slam that door on its insolence
and turn to resume your place at dinner, where civilized
manners still prevail? An inarguable commandment
from the colluding king demands its admittance. This voice
overrides your fastidious will with its prissy
parental fidelity to promise, its reminder that you
are not quite sovereign here. The frog writes its morse
of slime across your floor. It squelches into your elegant
dining room, demands to be lifted up to the table, soils
    irredeemably
the white linen cloth, reiterates the petulant chant of its
    demands.
You hear beneath its requests for a meal
a lewd implication of foot pads planted upon your hips,

its tongue aiming and adhering to every morsel of your skin.
And now you watch, repulsed, its feeding from your plate,
its glaze of mucous on your every mouthful.
You're ordered to carry it into your bedroom. A child again,
you have no choice. Croaking with its legends
of criminal lust, sucking in the world from both sides of its
     head,
it is a transgression of all that your clean
ordered life has attained. You plunk it
in a corner, hoping that at last you have bought
its silence. But it will not stop croaking in the foul
     presumption
of its claim to your person. It solicits a ghoulish
inter-species friendship, a bestial liaison that would leperize
your skin, breed in you some hellish spawn. You foresee
the bloom of its stains in your bed, its ignominious
discharge that will never be erased. It tells you to place it
onto your sheets. It tells you to undress. It is,
you are almost certain, swelling. You foresee waking
to the single eye of the sun with this frog like a tumour
protruding from your flesh. And you think:
Pay it back now while no one's looking.
Give it a childhood's unstinting vengeance.
You know already the sure satisfaction
of its splat on the wall, the ooze and inertness
that will christen its silence and leave you unmolested
in your own clean bed. You cup it like a baseball in the hatred
of your hand. You pitch to its instant extinction
this lump that has no business in your life.
You hurl the odious beast at the wall.
You slam it hard and watch what slides from that impact
to the floor. There, in place of the terminal Rorschach
of its viscera, is the still moist skin of a stunned
and raw unfolding beauty, the flesh of your most

fervid dreams. What appears, unclad
and unthinkable, is the purely pornographic answer
to your lusts. You gawk at this prince, this virile
beauty brewed in the algaed muck of the pond.
You wonder if these lustrous hypnotic eyes can be believed
when he attests that only your own precise aim and anger
could have spun him on the pivot of flesh and redemption,
and brought this freshly hulled body to light.
And you wonder in conundrums that will never
be resolved: Who was the witch who cast him
to such a repulsive and handy form? Who made you
the hater and pitcher and saviour of the sacred?
You have been blessed, you can see, by your fierce
indignation. It is your unbridled disgust he's required, your
    refusal
to submit to his viscous advances. He is standing now
in pulsing nakedness before you. You
approach him, moisten your lips; roused,
you acquiesce to the petals of his kiss.

The Little Mermaid

I

The troubles begin – for the mermaid and me –
with the fall of an image that arrests
our breath. Hers is a statue, a marble body
that plunges through fathoms of ocean to find her.
She's converted in that petrifying moment of beauty,
that planting of illicit love for a foreign species.
A first gaze gave form to my vague unease –
that drifting on childhood's map of gender –
slipped my foot to the unforgiving slipper of desire.
At fourteen an athlete stole my equilibrium,
bewildered my blood. He excited me with what
I knew I could not have, a burgeoning taste for what
I was not built for. The statue rests before her watered eyes,
the lineaments of disaster written in its face.
They were nothing we chose. The statues found us.

II

One day she sights on the deck of a ship a perfect man.
It was a Tuesday in August. I was nineteen.
He was, beyond description, beautiful – a prince
and my ticket to a childhood of stories. She needs him
like salt, that clamouring in her bones, can't deflect
her needs to more suitable partners, the local merboys
who frolic beneath her field of vision.

She would rather marry catastrophe than accept second best.
Resolved to fashion some religion from his beauty,
I would have him or nothing less than his image.

I worked in his light each long day that summer.
I gazed and adored and needed to change –
for I was not the kind he would marry.
As she hovers each night by the side of his ship,
hoping for a glimpse or the peal of his laughter,
she knows that her body is unsuitable, wrong.
She will yield to that brutal imperative: change.

III

We knew that our altering would not come without cost.
We knew of terrible bargains in darkness, of deformations,
infections. We darted down the tunnel
to the sea witch's cave, past the hallucinatory groping
of tentacled claws. We were ready
to forfeit any features we could barter. This
for the mermaid was the exorbitant price:
being sliced like a fillet from the fin of her tail
and hanging her voice like a plum on a tree.
Her body, unnaturally, is split clean open.
Having weighed the merits of castration
and suicide, I too would surrender whatever
was required. Silence seemed an acceptable price,
not for happiness but for some gambled chance
of its arrival. Our bodies were altered,
compromised, torn, my voice
withered to a tiny dried fruit in my throat.

IV

The prince was at once too innocent and virile
to admit me to the manly chambers of his passion.
He saw me as a faintly inexplicable friend
and never quite scented the note of my origin.
The mermaid, by the beseeching phrases of her eyes,
attempted to mimic the music left hollow in her throat.
She danced as on knives in her piercing silence,
felt not water but fire in the flick of her toes.
The prince loved her as an orphan, a page boy,
a pet. She basked in an affection
that chilled her to the bone. It was not
unexpected, though it knifed us again,
that our prince should choose a more natural mate.
We were, neither one of us, fish nor flesh,
and our mutilation did not match the prince's taste.

V

The mermaid and I were devoted to tragedy.
We could not proceed as our bitter
sisters entreated and murder the living image
of beauty. And finally, what's the choice
for a broken mermaid who has left behind him
the waters of his home to dance
at the feet of some man who rejects him?
What the mermaid has wanted is not above all
the bed of a prince but a loftier world
to which she might rise. We are given another
in a series of lives, becoming children of some still
further dawning. And our hunger for beauty
continues unappeased. The gorgeous forms a liquid

fire, draws us to its ever more rarefied air,
where the voice of our yearning is restored to our throats.
And there is nothing that so much tears and exalts us
and propels us again beyond the borders of our world.

35

The Bears' House

She spies it there naked and vacant as a cranium, tiptoes to
peek through the window of its eyes, surveys the bland
cozy cottage of family. She presses the door that unlatches
        before her,
proceeds in near archeological stillness, savours
the trespass on abandoned lives. Her story is simply
that no one is home. Bowls still steam with the slow
thoughts of morning, scroll a familial invitation on the air,
and the grey awaits the probings of her spoon.
A father's fury is raised to her mouth, strikes at her palate
with the sting of shame, brands and coffins
a corner of her tongue. Her taste of the mother is cold as a
        corpse,
freezes the running of thoughts in her veins, chills her
to a statue of girl and spoon. The baby's bowl gives her
the grey taste of childhood, of nearly congealed and
glutinous memory, a neutrality malleable, just, and right.
But the mass of its comfort cannot equal her hunger.

For solace she seeks the arms of the father –
but the heart of his chair is steely as a mirror, its wood as
        stony
and unyielding as a creed. She sinks to the welcoming
miasma of the mother where she'd be absorbed by the slow
tract of slumber, that soothing and ruminant placebo of
        peace.
She shakes herself free from these opiate florals, descends
to the perfect Platonic chair. It fits her like the slick grey
        glove
of thought, and she for one blessed moment is home.

But what's just and right will not support her.
It crumples and shards like a tree house beneath her; she's
    splayed
in the twigs of her grounded nest, abandons the wreckage
in her search for rest. She drifts
through the unclouded alembic of their lives, detects no wisp
of their bruinish wills, enters the still inner room of their
    sleep.
The first bed smells of sour male sweat, tastes
of all the cold minerals of the mind, and she lies here alert
as a casket in church. The next smells of lavender, washing,
and extinction; she's buoyed on the billowing white of its
    pillows, rocks
on the swells of unvisioned sleep, her body suppurating
like sweating pearls. She assays the hybrid
of baby's bed with its quilted panes of human pictures. She
    rests
where the skull of a bear has lain, senses its snout within
her own, and warmed by coverings that blend with her skin
melts toward the hive and honey of his dreams.

When the morning term of their exile is ended, the bears
spy their violable home through the branches, gingerly
cross the charged line of its entrance. When they see the
    bowl licked

clean of breakfast, the sticks lying splintered in a corner of
    the room,
they bristle with the furry thickness of their fortune, amazed
that so much of their lives remains. They won't wake this girl
with her cereal breath who lies here white as a black bear's
    shadow:
without the whiff of her human scent their noses might
    never
have compassed them home. She has preserved by her
    curious
presence the lives they'd let fall like hot spoons from their
    mouths.

The Eldest Dancing Princess

In the cabinet of her chamber are the branches
snapped like rifle fire from the trees of that life:
the leaves of silver, gold, crushed diamond –
greyed now with a delicate layer of dust.
She once knocked on every stick of this bedroom's
dead furniture – but it would not corkscrew
to the floor at her feet, yield a stairway to a land
with its own spangled sky. The soldier
was an old man then and is older now.
He deprived her of her one prophylactic
against aging: the sparkling eyes of that prince
in his perennial youth, his gaze that never measured
the fading of her face, his nightly erasure
of her accumulating years. She remembers
how he matched her desire with the underworldly
precision of wishes. And when she was encircled
in his arms, her feet were infallible in the rhythms
of the dance. Now her life slides beneath a single shared
     moon,
and she has no admittance to where deeper constellations
wheel above her. She no longer descends to where beauty
awaits her and she is lavished with the praise of a prince's
tongue. She has waited beside the whisper of bedsheets
for the throat of the chthonic to cry out her name –
but found only the silence of this wooden world. In the bed
of her clever if diffident soldier she has not found
a suppleness or fineness of waist, any semblance
of her prince's lissome grace. She esteems
in him all the plainness of daylight, his hands marked
with the dark of this world's sure machinery. And here

in his sturdy unmannered affection she has learned
a dimension of waking she had never set hope on.
His eyes in their earthly absence of the marvellous,
their flecks the shades of soil and stones,
glitter as with a deep unsmelted ore. And there can be
no replacement of what she has lost. Long ago
she was given the gift of a thousand nights
of magic with a prince unsurpassed in refinement
and beauty. Now this humble world has kneeled,
proposed, and she, with unparalleled elegance
mausoleumed in memory, she has accepted.

The Conception of Gautama

It's in dream that the marvellous is conceived
in the world. A stellar whiteness announces
its arrival, and a miracle of magnitude fills
her womb; a radiant white elephant, a toddling
child, steps coolly and easily into her side.
This benign, untutored, ingenuous step could
crush her with eagerness, innocence, white;
destroy her with its soft unpractised gait.
A trusting dazzlement curls and settles
itself in her belly, and she knows no tales
to comprehend this ingress, this perfect
and perplexing gift of violation. And she accepts
her impossible part in the birth of the world:
that she is the site and the soil
of paradox, the enfleshment of a vastness
she could never keep hidden, the footprint
and fresh cradling place of the sacred. She is simply
the soft earthly vessel where a great
and circling planet is nurtured. Her body
is frescoed with glistening murals,
lit with lambent elephant aurora. She carries
a new millennium deep within her skin. A young elephant's
shimmering has entered her flesh, and she learns
that she may be filled with an infant light
and still, with the world poised inside her, live.

Annunciation, Swimming

He is swimming and knows himself quick in his limbs,
his skin all slick with coolness and pleasure.
He is swording through water riveted with light,
and the world, the water, calls him by name,
announces that he is to be water's mother.
And he tells this god, this liquid: *No.*
I am not a candidate to conceive a new world.
I am, if you'd peek beneath my swimsuit, male.
But this aqueous god, accustomed to finding smooth paths
around resistance, won't take no for an answer.
He is four shades too ardent, a bright cadence with a plan,
a mystery who thrills to confound those it loves.
The world will admit itself to your skin
stir like a word in your clearest pools
and flicker with the quickness, the spear flash, of minnows.
He is stripped by the lickings and lappings of this god,
adored by the face and force of adoration.
He is bred with the shimmer and brilliance of wet–
and the liquid he glides through is the liquid he'll bear.
He's become the abundant generation of swimming,
and plundered by water, cannot say where he ends.

A Wish to be Mary

Every gay man harbours a wish to be Mary,
to say, *Let it be done to me*
according to your will. Each of us wishes
to be blackened as a man beneath a raptor's
broad wings, to shiver in the eclipse
of the plummeting God. We would,
like Mary, be asked for our nearly
irrelevant consent. We would be mastered
by the force of the holy and taken
by that potency more than human
or male. We would have shadows printed
on each of our organs and know
that intemperate pressure tattooed
as bruises into our flesh. We would admit
that wild beating plumage, the sharp
fierceness of air, the descending strike
of transgression, devastation, bliss.
The visions and imaginings of every
gay man are a foretaste of that moment
when divinity thickens from cloud into flesh,
and we're the stunned half-resistant
victims of a will that makes itself lord
of all our terrain. And no beauty exceeds
the thrilled muscle of blindness
in that exalting erasure when the savagery
of God renders us each a cipher,
a vanishment, a saint. We all crave
in a swelter of religious need to be chosen
and sought by the spinner of spheres, to be cruised
and pursued and reduced by brute strength.

We all want to be seared by the need of God,
to have this night blazoned with the mark
of pure scalding, to be wreaked
with a blessing that exceeds human shape.

And Then When We Enter

And then when we enter the body of God,
hushed by this feathered unexpected
unfolding of wings, we're aghast and allured
by the gender of the world, our desires
grown wider than we'd ever conceived.
We accept her beckoning though we have
no right, and we're drawn to this beauty
all gloaming, uncloaking, and flow, a smooth
river of blackness sweet with the scent
of pears and dark berries. We plead that this
is a feat that we are not made for, that our bodies,
our spirits, were not fashioned for this.
And in the face of her blandishments, we submit
to this clear masculine sacrament that we have never
had occasion to learn. Overcome by this sure
reshaping of our wills, we know that anything less ardent
than what we commit would be a stark
betrayal of our blood. Our bodies,
in their every smoothed finger of moistness
and want, might be tears of emptiness, tears
of myrrh, might be tears of all our forgotten
losses. And with these we enter the body of God.

Erl-King

A figure robed in sheen of black
    Plucks my puling infant self.
He comes as an erl-king, an unwelcome saint,
    Lifts me and swings me to the roll of his shoulder.
And there's no one I could be said to be:
    There's him with this package of grief on his back.
He strides through a night that knows no naming,
    And I am too young, too small, too cold
To anyway alter the course of his feet.
    He walks until walking has been all of my life,
And there is in me no one who knows where we are:
    No one who could hope to find my way back.
I am merely a sorrow on the road to my drowning.
    At the end of this unending night he pauses,
Standing over water it would kill me to enter.
    It is black as oil and animal blood,
Water that transfixes and that I cannot read.
    I feel him soothing me down toward sleep;
He would do this as gently as tucking me in.
    From out of my softening bundle of slumber
There issues a voice unfamiliar – mine:
    I will not go a single step further.
I will not die as young as I am now.
    And he is powerless here to accomplish
What I had thought his unalterable task.
    He's abducted me again from my ordinary days,

Brought me to this bounty of black reaching waters;
    And as I scry the darkness he's singing –
Singing in a voice that offers no comfort,
    That holds me and unlatches the brimming black.

Krishna in the Desert

Sand has scoured
every word from his skull, robbed
him of any remembrance
of joy – and all colour has spilt
from the cups of his eyes.
He's misplaced
the lovely cool ring
of his name, and when the skies
cry out with his own
blue vowels, he hears only gibberish
scribbled on the wind.

And Garuda comes rushing
like a great golden dream, an eagle
all talons and sword-eyes and silk.
He comes like an angel where angels
are extinct, a swooping swift brilliance
from a vacant sky. He finds Krishna
collapsed and abandoned by beauty, his brain
stripped of all its articulate fabric
and blistering mutely in the rage of the sun.

As fondly as a father, Garuda recalls
each hair that has shone
on his treasured one's forearms, the joy
he's watched slumbering in the play
of these lips. Garuda has alighted
like a dream before Krishna, invites him
as a weary, expended child – and Krishna
plunges to the pillowed strength that is Garuda
like a man embracing a lake of gold.

He nestles among feathers scented
faintly with his tears, vaguely
remembers the flavour of water, and some
notion of ascent newly nudges
at his brain. Garuda's feathers
are smooth as a second skin,
and Krishna inhales their aroma of flight.

In their sleekness he hears
the pattering of water, splashing
its luscious abundance on his face;
feels it cleansing the length
of each strand of his hair. They rise
in a rapid crescendo of wings, soar
toward a distant, attending land
where water will course and gurgle and surge
with all the rippling cadence
of music, and words tumble
like birdsong from the blue one's throat.
With the colours of Krishna's eyes
washed clean, he will swim
in the palace and pool of his name, exulting
in the sparkling world that he is –

and holding always, an
infinitesimal treasure in his brain, one
harsh and gritting grain of sand.

Lament

I ask again how you in your ordering
Can have left these stretching pools of ordure,
This foulness that mars creation's face.
You've watched as I've been mired in the vilest of myself,
Destroyed by my own slow acid survival.
You've watched as I've been replaced by a vacant loathing.
Where in this battering blackness is your face?
And why do all the postures and recitations of attendance
Yield no light, no hope, no respite
From the death demon squatting, spawning on my chest?
A single word of comfort would sustain me –
A word that repeatedly does not come.
Though I listen and listen you will not speak.
You will not approach the husk of my life.
I ask again what I now doubt, that I will have strength
To resist the ineloquent wish for extinction
And wring from its visit some usable speech.
I remember with an uninhabited faith
The gifts you have scattered over my days,
All of them dried to ashes in my mouth.
Everything I have learned of you has been stolen.
I have woken decrepit and glittering with anger,
Detesting a world where such thievery inheres.
And once, cracking into my skull,
The words, absurd, that you need me to endure this,
That a tiny branch of your brain would crumble
Were I to lie down in this blankness and sleep.
And the words come clothed in such impotent sorrow
That I grieve for your sore and grieving voice.

Saul at Ramah

King Saul with his army is advancing
on Ramah, where in one stroke he will kill
his harp-boy and prophet. But Saul
is unable to enter the city, can step
inside it no more than he could lift
the lid from his skull and pluck at will
its pearly glands. As he approaches,
the God door opens at the base
of his brain, there is no floor
to support his thoughts, and he is to his horror
far more than himself. He views the stale
world in livid contortions, as through the clear
flowing windows of a prophet's mind – and it
teems at once on both sides
of his eyes. God speaks to Saul
through Saul's commandeered voice, throws him
in a flailing bewilderment of rapture –
the hive of his brain swarming
thickly with words, and honey
drooling out from the corners of his mouth.
His speech is thick with religion's
gruel and pours from his mouth
as he suffers the storming grand mal
of his God. He babbles
and drips like an infant or oracle
as the fist of God's voice assaults
and hammers and disgorges
his will. The invasion of God
has ransacked his manhood,

left him naked and squalling and
writhing on the road, his brain scrambled
by the curious fingers of his God –
and stained by the vomit of unhuman words.

Death's Invitation

On the day I was born, a generation of poets
was lining up for suicide: soaking in the century's
virulent oils and igniting themselves in a fury
of anguish. This is the horoscope
I cannot escape, death's
invitation pinned to my stars.

I imagine a yielding to the shades in my blood,
a taking of my place in suicide's queue.
I imagine diving in conclusion
into myself, that shimmering green glimpse
of a crow's closing wing, the snapping shut of the one
brief book of my speech. I imagine all the genes
of my thoughts vacated from the world, the dissolution
of that negligible fragment of dialect. And this
is a loss that I cannot allow – determined
that my life will not end
in advance of what count as my requisite words.

Sheltering this stubborn, unfoundable resolve,
I protect my suicide voice from extinction.
I resist the cries that rake my skin for longer
than I believe I can, enduring till despair
lays down its savagery and briefly relents
to speak itself through me.
And who is this darkness
who hungers to know itself
on my tongue, who pummels me for days, steals
each sliver of joy, repeats its unanswerable
will to erase – then smears my lips

with the liquids of its mouth, singing
of a world that can barely endure its surfeit of beauty,
that admits us and counts us among its own
only as we gamble the whole price of our skin?

Captives

That flesh could so immensely inhabit itself – these bodies
so compacted with atoms of will – and breathe as stone
breathes the densest of light. This motion is utterly

what their lives are made of – and the mind continues
the sculptures' turning, sustains that taut and urgent
petalling, that sensuous extension toward what impels them.

They command an ascent I have hardly begun, this
crystallization of flesh into light – and they offer no rest
among stone's vocation. By their physical grace I submit

to this change – to make of myself an icon of motion,
twisting till I'm lit by their smooth, giant beauty –
till I adore and exceed myself as purely as stone.

Two Boys on a Riverbank

How the world is slivered to its requisite
    colours, the land in these attentive hands
        restored to its soft and summoning
mother of pearl. Here, where colours
    unveil their smooth undersides of light,
        is a benediction steady as rain,
a splashing of gratitude to the canvas
    of our eyes. In this delicate severing
        of the earth to its moments, paint shimmers
to doorway to permit us to pass – to walk
    where acres of quiet and birdsong await
        our feet as we step sole and companioned
under canopies of sky. The present proceeds
    in its blurred interlacing of pink flowering
        and mauve, a story that assembles us
footstep by footstep, and breeds in us
    its cool palettes of air. We are
        this invention of indelible light, of a sun
that strikes brilliance to the river
    of our lives, and are rich in the cool
        iridescence and shadow, in the breeze
that washes and welcomes our breath. We sieve
    the river's song to its notes, lapped
        by its fresh and unbroken adoration, and enter
this clearing that yields its plenitude of light.
    And here every leaf of our lives
        is of beauty, as precious as fingers
of branchlight and stem. A painting
    we might have passed with a glance,
        the world beckons us, patiently, unable

to conceal its soft handfuls of bloom.
    And we follow its trails of treeshade
        and calm to where light at last
will reveal its intentions and we'll witness
    what the riverbank holds in its breath,
        this devout and earthly investiture of air.

Muhammad and the Moon

He stands at the base of a column of moonlight
    And camels kneel before him.
And again as he gazes on a new revelation
The sky as he's known it breaks into bits,
The moon parting as bread into crumbs of white.

Muhammad has observed how the heavens are sundered
How they need the press of human thought
To restore them toward an unfractured whole.
    And camels kneel before him.
The moon, like a soul, like a flock in a tree,
Is a delicate assembly inclining to shards.

And when it is puzzling in the night above us
And scripture is a scattering of luminous fragments
That form no trail, no hope of home,
The moon floats broken as the heart of God
And calls those who see it to the work of mending.

Muhammad is a desert then, praying for rain.
    And camels kneel before him.
He knows that the moon is remade like words,
The rounding of verses to curve and sphere.
He knows that our feast must float whole in the heavens
So that light might complete every crevice inside us –
Healing our fissures as we're smoothed in its hands
And making us pitchers to sail white through the sky.

Water runs from the thirst of Muhammad's fingers,
And the moon is the giving clay he forms.

Muhammad as a child shapes the yielding light:
Turning it until it again takes wing,
Until we see the circle of its awestruck face
As it steers unassisted through the dark of the sky.
    And camels kneel before him.

Hunters

On the rooftop, dazed
as a lizard in the noonday sun,
Peter prays, his white eyes
on God. Dyslexic with hunger,
he sees descending from heaven a billowing
sail. Inside it swarm all the creatures
of Earth, a sinuous teeming knot
of flesh, a writhing
of the kinds that stepped
and slid and scuttled from the ark. Peter salivates
for the meats he'd eat roasted for lunch,
the sail draped like a napkin beneath
his meal. God nudges and abets his appetite:
Get up, Peter, kill
and eat. Peter's in a quandary of hunger
and uncleanliness. God craves
sweet blood, the scent
of roasting in famished nostrils, splashes
in red on Peter's brain a vast
unkosher scene of butchery.

As the forest before him crashes
into flame, Krishna's eyes flicker with private
need. In a thunder of running,
the forest disgorges
all of its beasts. And Krishna,
replete from his picnic, effects
the massacre Peter imagined, warring
on the fire's refugee flood. He pierces
the trembling stalks of windpipes, extinguishing

with his discus and arrows, his bow
replenished like an automatic weapon,
the animals frenzied and driven by heat –
clambering over the moraine of carnage
as they hurl themselves from fire
to blade. It's not about meat
but the quick plunk and pleasure
of well-aimed death. Krishna's toes
sink deep to the ooze of soil, his calves
two small islands in his own red sea.

When Peter and Krishna finally meet beneath the sign
of heaven's butcher, Peter hefts the old keys
from his pocket, and pushes open the gate
of the door. As they step inside
to the moisture and cool, they're met by the eyes
of leopards and lambs, carcasses
hanging like flowers from the ceiling's hooks.
The cases are packed
with pig hooves, chameleons, hands
of chimpanzees, tigers' genitals, the brains
of lions, seals, and skunks. The men stand
delirious in the morgue-like air. The corpses turn
in the sleeping cool trays of their display, pressing
to joints of shoulder and hip their crutch-like
legs; assembling their cuts and trails
of offal, the partly pickled
onions and coils of their brains. They hobble
with half-limbs over the counter
and creep across the polished floor.

Neither Peter nor Krishna is hungry now.
The animals claim restitution of their skin,
torn from damp garbage or someone's

shoes, patched and corroded
and bearing gold buckles, pelts splayed
on their flesh like bikinis and stoles. Surrounded
by manged and cobbled animals, hides geographic
with trimming and tuck, some
missing hoof or ear or tongue,
Peter and Krishna cringe unarmed,
unprotected by mantra, dagger, or bow.

The animals shuffle like impatient
patrons, stumble like puppets
in their ill-fitting limbs. They wait
for the mouths of Krishna and Peter, mouths
that never fountained with their own dark blood,
to expound the theology of animal
killing, and how the gods love
to lap new-spilt blood.
The sailcloth in Peter's mind wrings with red.
Krishna feels blood rising high on his thighs.
The animals lick their scarred lips
and bleat, patient
as appetite and the craving for meat.
They want to taste like the salt of prayer
the finely religious pleasures of the kill.

Jesus and Buddha Commiserate

How eager they have been to peel us out of the human
    sphere
and hurry us into the realm of legend: exacting on us a
    desperate
elevation that renders us harmless. They would steal a
    man's life
as an idol to polish, smearing us with a reverence that
    leaves us
irrelevant, and dissolves us into some useless nirvana.
It is as if each of us, discouraging clinging, left their minds
with nothing to grasp. And if only they had persisted
with that nothing, the silent gulf beyond what they know.
Now we've left them relying on our dead merit, the
    precarious
vicarious where they balance their lives. Somehow we've
    replaced
what we sought to pull down. Sometimes I think
our suicide might do them good, might yank them
out of their childish reliance. But of course it was us or
    someone
else, religious minds in their youth abhorring a vacuum.
I'd save them, I've thought, myself, if I could: infect them
with a hunger to invent the holy. I would wash them clean
of their punishing attachments, leave them floating free
of all their small certainties. How thrilling it would be
to see some rookie seize the ball, sprint and deke as I did in
    my prime,
blazing a way down religion's bright field.
Or pose me koans that stretch me to bursting; refute me
with parables that embarrass my own. What I'd give

for a brash religious surprise, a phrase or a story that rattles
my teeth, awakens my organs to gasp at its beauty, its
    shattering
and recasting of an outworn world. I remember, when
    again inclined
to despair, that what bit us is still a creature with teeth.

Mating Our Faiths

We have tasted the bodies of other religions,
been stained by that fierce and animate adultery,
and there is no purity to which we could return.

We bear the winking pearls of others' pleasure,
the tiniest rubies and sapphires of a line.
We suck the subtle nectars of discovered gardens

and transport rare pollen on the fur of our feet.
We carry the powders of praise in our hair,
bathe in pools slick with the juices of love.

We are glazed with creation's consecrated fluids,
bear a novel abundance of pheromones and genes.
We are a field, a sower, a scattering, and seeds.

We want the one life each religion yearns for:
we want to heal the wide fissures that mar the world.
We want our day's faithful promiscuous prayer,

its precious religious erotic revelation.
We step toward a long unprophesied future
with acts our ancestors would revile and shame.

We are that unanticipated moment when ancient borders
    fade
from maps, when wisdom meets wisdom with unbridled
desire, when beauty with beauty is free to breed.

Radha and the Beloved Disciple

That among the delirious hordes who adore him
The pulse of his body would be pulled toward us.
That our forms would accord with the desires of his heart.

That those eyes that have shone before the sun
Should perceive this particular beauty in us,
Hold us as the place where their gaze might rest.

To be chosen like a single grain in the marketplace,
To be plucked like a pearl from the depths of the Earth –
To know we fit to him as cup to hand.

We wish to curl in the ribbon at the centre of his eye,
To be burned in his nearly annihilating love,
To become the centre for the centre of the world.

Generations will place themselves in our skin
To know through our nerves the body of the holy,
To be in us lovers of all that is.

No proscription could hold us from the boldness of his arm,
No notion of decency deter us from his touch.
For him we would forsake all we have been taught.

Each of us would blissfully trade decades of rectitude
For the scandal of meeting his beauty by evening,
The gratitude of knowing him illicit in the night.

Imageless Image

When all that was the precious gift of religion bathes
the air, a smashed jar
of perfume; and all those figures we have most
adored have melted
to the imageless image of God, to an immaculate nothing
that pools all about us;
then the light we have loved, that poured itself freely
through the lines
of story and song – that light will not leave us orphaned.
A spring will arise
to quench us with words, to enliven us with vision, impulse,
and verse. We will wake
in an intricate unstudied language that we by our birthright
know how to speak. We will share
as we share the marrow of trees the dreams that flood us
like a raven's wing.
And all that held itself in silence will dive from the water
wet with song. And that light
who left us dipped in divinity's pigments, it will be
as a bird that sweepsand carols, gathering and condensing
    the blue of the sky.
It will be.

The Fisherman's Wife

After her audacity in asking to be God,
she sits alone in her hovel's kitchen, enthroned
again on her worn wooden stool. She is clad in the
    sumptuous
bolts of poverty, and her skin is innocent
now of brocade. None of the papacy's
luxuries surround her, none of that extravagance of roast
    lamb
and quail, that giddy glitter of gem on gem. All authority
has fallen like sceptres and ringed keys from her hands.
No one bows, obsequious, before her, or plies her ears
with hymns of praise. There are only
the pots, the ladle, the knife, the old chipped plates
and well-worn bowls. There is merely this humble gallery
of dailiness and use. And she has only pity
for bishop, king, and pope. She wonders
if her boldest request has not been granted, if God
has not seized her inveterate greed and used it
to lure her precisely here. She wonders if the eyes surveying
this scene are not God's. And whose eyes but God's
could wash the world in such lemony light? Her hut in all
its stark simplicity is still riveted tight
and ribboned with inextinguishable light. This ritual
peeling and eyeing of potatoes, this repeated
chopping of onions and carrots, this measured
heading and gutting of fish: is not this
the sustaining creation of the world? Her wish
to be no one less than God, to be nothing
less than everything that is – is not this
the largest, most generous, most forgivable sin? Is it not

the very sin that God would draw her toward, tugging
her desires past the brink of God's being? God's nostrils
delight in the scent of the blending
warm herbs of her soup. God is well pleased
with another day's work. And she
is redeemed with her every needle of avarice.

Sea of Ink

If all the trees of the earth were pens, and the sea,
replenished by seven more seas, were ink,
the words of God could not be finished still.

Qur'an 31.27

You dip to the flashing inkwell of the oceans
Your infinite quiver of forested pens.

You dip your array of supple nibs
To a liquid as dark and scriable as mind.

You pen phrases to flutter unceasingly in the ears of
    creatures,
Your profusion never bumping its hand against silence.

You are the interminably voluble God
Pouring out limitless versions of the world.

You have left us with bold and partial accounts,
The leavings and sloughings of revelation's drafts.

Entrusted with these notes toward an opus,
We lean breathless over your shoulder as you write –

Occasionally glimpsing our names in your script,
And daring to break into the street with news.

Continuing the Story

The story is unfinished – or who would we be?
Who would we be if the revelations were ended,
if salvation's fable were fully worked out and we
were marooned past the end-point of story?

The crux of our one earthly life is how we inherit
this unfinished manuscript: preserving its purity
by capping our pens or joining the ragtag ranks
of plagiarists and prophets. We might add
to the draft of the life of Christ, hurtling forward
the scenes he began, careting in
further words and phrases, marking up with our pens
this heirloom scripture we've received.
We make up what is missing in the colours
of Christ, in the peevishness, exuberance,
and visions of Christ, in the suffering and decrepitude
and delights of Christ, the spitting and scribbling
and poetry of Christ. This work is the very
novelty we offer to God, the pleasure
we might give in unprecedented speech.

Our intemperate hope is that the one reading
will tremble as the sheerest wing trembles
with change, mystery adjusting by a micron
its centre of gravity, turning by the merest
arc second the compass of its course. We make up
what is missing in the epic of Christ, beseeching
the words of our own, our only salvation.

Below Me in Blue

Below me, far
below me in blue,
is the pool's hardly bearable
geometry of water. And I
am no diver. I am here
in a lane floating high
above lanes, a pool
that peers down on this azure
pool – amazed no one else
chooses this height where I
swim – this giddy and spacious solitary
pool, where I swim in lanes,
my body in graced, instinctual
motion. I am swimming above
a bewilderment of blue –
and far below that pool
is another – water hidden
beneath water as gold
within gold, a lensing and laddering
I can't see the end of.
I have swum in each one
of the pools below me, known its water
cool and blue on my limbs,
given thanks as it parted its skin
to receive me. I have known
my body anonymous, devoted
to motion, not knowing which
of the pools I'd returned to.
And I live in a world of infinite
water, water on water

spanning up through the sky,
where not one among us
has the right to be.
I live among rungs
of blue and swimmable air, jewels
that cannot cease to glint
and beguile me, that covet and invite
the glide of my swim.

Guru Nanak and Jesus

They've been washed in what is unpartisan, wet,
burst spraying from the pool of cool religion.
They see the skies cut open by wings, feel the heavens

embrace them as they rise from water. They are filled
past brimming with a waking giddiness that slips
itself blissfully under their skin – a cavorting that upends

all they have been taught. They are naked, unencumbered,
plunging to be born again and again.
They know that the first is the only number –

repeating, like infant or imbecile: one.
They have entered a revelation so broad
it admits no heresy. Their bodies

are the bridge between religions, phrases
scatter with the drops from their hair, and they're
christened as madmen, prophets, saints.

They're the place where again the water is born.
Their lips a benevolence as generous as clouds,
they cast the seeds and the ragas of joy.

Wise as sages and ebullient as boys,
they feel their beings threaded through with song.
They are startled to find themselves

inside God's body, startled they have never
been anywhere else. They have heard
the water, and the answer is one.

And nothing could convince any listeners to subscribe
to their folly, to this mad, uncontainable mode of knowing.
They each could sing for the remainder of their days

from what they are given in this fluid moment.
What they teach is only water's lesson:
dive deeper, hold your breath, ring death's doorbell,

and you'll see that there is only one –
and one so spinning and incipient with joy –
it tosses us an exuberance we cannot lay down.

Krishna and Jesus in Algonquin Park

They hoist their canoe to the lichened rocks
and face the smooth light they've paddled across.

Shucking the weight of their pale-coloured clothes
and plunging to the knuckly cupped hand of the lake,

they meet in the green, share their scents with the water,
feel their bodies enlivened with cool liquid sensation,

and turn in the still black waters of their minds.
As they ripple the mirror between world and world,

each sights the stroking phantoms of the other's limbs,
and touches skin as papery smooth as birch.

They climb the smoothed ladder of rocks at the shore,
their abdomens slick and quick with their breath,

and lie with their backs baked sweet with stone.
Blue and clouds tumble to creation in their eyes.

Leading each other down pine-cooled trails,
the air sultry with blueberry and warm golden grasses,

they step to the island's needled shade,
and each scents the lake-sweet on the other's skin.

When evening has come and their hungers are sated,
their senses warmed by the perch where they sit,

their thoughts float calm as loons on the water –
then plunge to surface, later, someplace else.

Their bodies as languid as the swaying of trees,
they listen to the applause of breeze in the aspens,

know the touch of each star as it plays on their skin,
and lie down in the circling of heavens on earth.

Place

Meandering as a tourist among the remnants
of what I consider the natural world, I'm opaque
to whatever it might have to say. A member of my vainly
autistic generation, I have lived for too long in exile
from place and lost what might be moved
by natural beauty. Diffident on that prickling question
of whether I can yet effect a return, I keep walking
through this range of unnamed trees, stretching my senses
toward their limits of attention, coaching myself
to what should be woven like blood within me: being
in this body as it walks in the world.
And on the path there is a turtle, a patience
anciently and stonily not me, yet so full of sense
and internal plotting, so fully at home
on this one patch of earth, that I stand in the wonder
and the gaze of its weight. I watch it taste
the coolness of air on its extremities, watch the glass
of its nearly immobile eye, watch it bask
in the sun on this path until this being in its rigour begins
to eclipse me. Then it steps like prehistory into
the brush. And rinsed in this meeting, I
am beginning to be in this place, a witness
to its summoning green and flutter, here
among trees and marsh and bantering
birds. A yellow finch
darts with a glee I nearly remember, and I begin to hear,
like air on skin, what a life simply
lived on this Earth might be like. There's
a murmur, still barely discernible, that invites me
to leave this exile I have been and move
toward a land that the land will show me.

That the Stars

Who am I that the stars have been lost to me?
Who am I that their languages of light
are not mine? Who am I who on this cold
crackling night am pinned beneath the clear
material heavens? I have allowed the blunting
of my senses, the routine flensing
of starlight from my skin. This quiver
of brilliance invites me to return, to be
the one held and to be beholder.
I spin below the gaze of a knowing
that has waited and wished for me patiently
for years, and there's no shading of blame
on this face that fills me. Now to be here
beneath the querying silence of stars, to hear
the curved space of the accompanying
sky, to be lit in every nerve
with this attending light. And who am I
who am granted this again, that this unearthly
precision might again be uttered to my eyes?

Kayaking the Vézère

After passing a few fishermen, I
was alone. A luminous blue hummingbird
swept over the river. Herons
spread great grey-blue wings to proceed
before me. And for paddle on paddle,
moment on moment, there was no
other human on the river or its bank
and I was alone with an older
world. And I spoke
to this place, to its tremor and pulse,
to trees and river and reaching rock.
I spoke from a body sorely filled
with longing, and uttered
the nameless address of the world, the *You*
that invokes the sheerness of relation.
And I sensed the stillness, the regard
of listening, that waiting on the water
among birdsong and branches. Something bent
in the sheltering curve of the trees and murmured
in the river's shimmering cadence. I might say
the world in it magnificence spoke –
for what else to call
that long-remembered swell in my chest, that
warm and tremulous skirring of wings, the feeling
like a child's when this life
is too much and I am at once all broken
and filled. It let me press my cheek
to its skirts, slide with my shoulders into
its current and take its deep
wild scent to my lungs. It gathered

around me, riffling me with breath, holding
me close in its gaze of elation. This place
had placed its hand upon me. And I was no longer only
human but more rocky and winged and
flowing and old. I was blue and jewelled
as a hummingbird whirring among
the multiple fingers of the trees. I was moving
through a world that held me
as nothing and loved me as deeply
as the fish and the falling leaf.

Driven to the Wilderness

What was dove and fluttering moments before
has hardened to a harpy that drives me
to this wilderness empty of human breath and bread.
It is on these harsh naked pages that scripture
will be stretched with the limits of my flesh. It is here
that I might be entrusted with the one next line
of that spiralling song. And here begins,
coeval with hope, the devilry of doubt:
that the Spirit would chart its course in me, conjure music
from this rattlebag junkheap of my heart. Welcome
to hunger, thirst, and heat. Welcome to a mind
whining thin and unfed. Welcome, dear friend,
to temptation. Temptation is no more than the wish
for the ordinary, for defection from this rank
absurdity of story, that image of a rift, a gash
in the sky. Temptation is simply the dismissal
of that transporting, epileptic moment of the call –
a call or a playing of light on the river. I am here
as a nearly normal man seduced by the fantasy
of a prophet's vocation. And there is
nothing here, no voice but the hollow vapid stuttering
of my own. If I am a prophet, I have nothing
to say. I look over wilderness empty as I am. And I am
an idiot, inserting myself in some chapter of scripture,
presuming that God would speak here – to me; presuming
that the reeling of the world has a voice, that my heart
might for a moment be tuned to receive it. I have opened
with listening an abyss of futility. And I long for death,
that strong salt drink, the only solution to this itch
in my soul, my brain, my belly. The food that my hunger

summons from memory and stone is as delicate
as petals in the muzzle of my mouth. There's a jackal
cackling through the curtains of night, shining
the well-oiled lamps of its eyes. A scorpion
teases with its coy approach, its willingness
to cast me to the flaming pit of its fever. I have known
the padding of patterned light footprints in my dreams, the deft
and almost timid inquisition of foxes as they gaze
on the mange of my nakedness, my rotting vegetal
concavity of face; as they sniff my stink of slippery
offal thinly wrapped in skin. I am questioned by
a venerable persistence of lizards, by that slick and wizardly
reptilian brain, know my sweat as a lemony flavour on the air.
The birds of carrion orbit the sweet fruit
of my eyes. I have been this bird, eager
for the bounty of my own death, for the residual lightning
of a newly stopped heart. I have torn at my own taut fibres,
stretching and snapping the elastic of my veins, tugging
each casing
of muscle from bone. I have known the viscous slippage
of this flesh from my mouth. I have wobbled on the precipice
of being human. I have known myself begin to fall, unsure
if there were wings to save me. There have been nights
and days and I cannot count them. There have been years
in the wilderness without hope or home. I have exposed
my idiot's vocation to the reckless unpardoning
interrogation of animal eyes. I have drunk of their wildness
and cannot but know the human stink of poverty
that coronas my soul. I have seen in the clear
undomesticated pitches of their eyes, in their bodies eidetic
with visions of dark, that they are the ones to shine
judgment

upon me, that I hold no greater trove of wisdom,
no prerogative to wrap the centuries in flesh. A pack of
    angels
cajoles me to act, to enter with stealth and creaturely
    cunning
my part in the kingdom where I am not king, my part
in the creeping, crepuscular family of God.

Raven and Jesus

Raven's been impatiently waiting for Jesus.
He is the dove's elder, foul-breathed brother.
He's the joke by which this world was spoken,
the rainbow where every colour is born
of black. He folds and unfolds his wings like duplicitous
scriptures. He will be the black stain rising sweetly
through scrolls of text. And if Jesus
thought that by water his sins were forgiven,
here's this flapping lump of mischief, this casual
virulence hopping over rock. Raven seeks no
confession, wants only to show how sins
can be mined. Jesus, observant, feels his arms
enraptured with the black apparatus
of wings. He samples the plundering irony
of a life without toil. Jesus digests Raven's lessons
like untrustworthy meat. And there
by night is Raven pecking flesh, pulling strips
from the hull of Jesus' chest, unwrapping the black tissue
that had hidden his heart. Raven tears the veil
between the chambers of Jesus' brain. He teaches Jesus
how to shrug free of the cape of himself, how to angle
a story so it's nearly invisible, so that no one
could extract its sliver from the skin.

All in All

We are saved, if at all, with every counted hair of our heads,
with each blooming of lichen, plankton, and light.
We are saved with each petal, apricot, bee,
with each one of the numbered and garrulous sparrows.
We are saved with the dense serenity of trees,
with each curl of damp and larval life.
We are saved, if at all, the way fields
are saved in each spade of their depths.

We are not plucked, as flowers from this world,
but lifted, if at all, with the mass of the planet,
its mantle and core the beating beneath us,
its steady respiration the rhythm we rise by.
This Earth reaches with us toward its florescence, yearning
for some future held out like a hidden season.

We are saved with the clear generosity of water,
with the air and sky that have always clothed us,
with the planet's long pageant of river and rock.
We are saved, if at all, with our ancestors' footprints,
with every enlightenment bestowed on our species,
with the grandeur and wreckage of all we have been.

The hopes of our birth are not extractable,
cannot flower and flourish apart from this soil.
We cannot be scavenged like filings
from dirt, like gold from gravel. No heaven
will admit us naked of Earth, our home's
wild wardrobe shorn from our skin.
We are welcomed, if at all, with the frailty

of this family we shepherd through illness,
with the sorrow of our elders sewn into our skin.

We are saved, if at all, with this palette
of flowers that we cannot be lifted to redemption
without. We are saved with the animal companions
who are the unsheddable body of our thought.
We are saved, if at all, with the minerals
in our bloodstream, the copper staining of dreams,
with the rivers of wisdom we are planted beside.

Magnificat

You who watch over the world's impossible births,
    you have not left the infertile to languish in shame
    but crept around the corners of procreation's codes.
You have drawn sap through brittle, desiccated branches,
    coaxing from the barren, the emasculate, the lame,
    from those ravished by incubus, angel, and djinn,
    what the paragons of the species could never produce.
You have drawn up from the pitiable dregs of the gene pool
    the progeny who will be emblazoned with future.
You have stolen history from the lips of the victors
    and crowned the reticent gene with approval.
You have fashioned an embryo perfused with your wish,
    lit the hopes of a seemingly final generation.
You have not forgotten your implausible promise
    first made to nameless expansion and fire,
    to that far floating dust that would become us,
    to the progenitors of sunlight, water, and green.
So great is your love for the daughters of water, the sons
    of soil, and so great is the place you have given
    to this generation, that ages to come might name us
    as the ones who kept the covenant with life –
    might forget us as any extinction securely averted.
You who rescue weary history with incarnations
    of surprise, you have not condemned us as our atrocities
    deserve, not consigned us to the dark of a muted future.
You have conceived within us a new narration,
    an infant and unsuspected pathway to peace.

Anointing

The Spirit of God has arisen within us.
It calls us by name and by remnants of text
    as it called to the waters and the earliest stars.
It entreats us to elaborate the thinly imagined
    good news to the poor, to cry comfort
    to the indigent indigenous players of creation:
To proclaim to trees, to fields and frogs
    that the God of their sap is suffering with them;
    that the world is still enamoured of their embattled
    profusion, of every leaf and toe of their kind.
The Spirit appeals that we lay down our arms,
    that we free all we've captured in our blanket of
    oblivion,
    and no longer claim the body of Earth as our spoils.
It announces an amnesty where we'll grant
    land the license to exceed its cramped ghetto,
    bring a release to the camps where animals languish,
    return to creatures the freedom to roam and to brood.
The Spirit is pleading that we preserve
    a wilderness where it may still speak, that the world
    might find within us a thicket of listening.
The Spirit calls us to be evangelists of beauty,
    apostles for all this world's visible marvels,
    inviting a generation opaque in their senses
    to trace the veins in the hands of trees,
    wait on birds whose orisons and lyrics we've unlearned.
It beckons us to open the book of its arts
    that the eyes of our hearts might open within us
    as the eyes of the trees reopen in spring.

The Spirit boldly proclaims that the Earth
    might yet emerge from the weight
    we've placed upon it, shake off the flakes
    of its moribund musings, and dazzle
    our eyes with the raiments of rebirth.
The Spirit plants within us the promise of a year
    when our debts to the Earth might be forgiven
    and we can meet with peace its unwavering gaze.
It dares us to imagine a day when life,
    this life, will express its favour, fan out again
    the deck of its treasures, and clothe us
    in the warmth of its dawning regard.

Continuing the Party

The party has swollen beyond what the fretting hosts
can afford, and they, in danger of a dry,
unshakable shame, have crouched
with their plea at Mary's ear. The news has everything
to do with her son, for his is always the party's hour.
And always the first thing Jesus will do
is ensure that celebration will not sputter to its end.
He hungers for the riot of this world to go on.
He wants, like any earnest hedonist, to know
the loosening of his body with dusk, the easing of strictures
that have bridled his mind. He wants the crush
of grape, the release of flavours, the delicious
slow drugging of a party's flesh. He'll summon an abundance
from the plainness in jars, a carpet of poppies
woven from water. The bride and bridegroom will be clasped
in happiness, and poverty will not cast
its shadow on their day or strike its acrid note
at marriage's start. Jesus will ensure that the guests
do not dribble out to the roads, not shut so soon
the crammed drawers of the night but circle and share
the dust of their shoulders, their bodies' soft pollen.
He will pour out the shine of human oil in firelight,
the lightness luring feet and fingers into air. He will thread
his intentions through them in drink, his crimson magic
warming their tongues and blessing their every mingling
     pleasure.
I ask this now for the water inside me.
I want to be clothed in the velvety
ribbons of wine, to bloom incarnadine
and be sipped in joy. I want to be emboldened

to what will permit the world to go on. I want
to invite the dancing with grateful oblivion
through the long granted night of our reprieve.

Mass

I

I address you, at odds with the tenor of my time;
stirred by an untraceable urge to engage you
with words and build in syllables some circuit
with creation. I am, with my restive generation, wary
of the delusions and atrocities, the gross embarrassments
that talk with you entails. A novice
in the complex grammar of prayer, I scavenge
among its atavistic arts, listening
for a cadence innate and nearly unknowable.
And with no surer way to span such infinite
intimate space, I launch toward you the crude craft
of my language, hoping that from this unfluent beginning
I might step toward the gloss of sacred speech.

I know you as the friction and frisson between silence
and speech, that papery rustling of wish into wish. I know
    you
as the easeful entry of a sleekness of thought, the caress
of mingled pigments on the parchment of my eyes, the
    laving
of a glacial freshness on brain and tongue. I know you
in your shivering visits to the plane of my flesh
when I am the guest of your plethora of beauty.
I know you in the moments of my plain life's
suspension when the smooth chords beneath it resound
unobscured. I know you in the underleaves of darkness
never fully revealed, the murmuring music of quotidian joy.

You are the robust celebration of my cells, the weight
of a blindness I almost can't bear, the sorrow that plunders
each harbour of my blood. You are the exquisite who flows
on both sides of my listening skin. You are
the thrill and caesura that hide within all names –
that polished emptiness pressing upon speech.

II

You who exceed our every notion of wholeness, whose
        vastness
we've fractured to brief scattered strains,
forgive us the cracking of this world
to our kindling, our indelicate severing of atom from song.
Forgive us for not daring to live by the deepest we know:
by those moments when a brilliance illumined our losses
and imprinted a fierce avid wonder on the lobes
of our brains; when we knew within us the width of the
        world –
that bright ladling of water to our thirsting hands.
Forgive us the riddling holes in our speech
and our silence, our accepting too readily a penury
of words, our failure to trace with requisite care
the arch and the ache of the wide sky inside us.

94

Forgive us our conclusion that you had expired,
the cosmos drained of its sweetness and soured
like milk. Forgive us our presumption that we know
who you are, that you might be discarded
on the thinnest of glimpses. Forgive us for cinching your
    stories
to closure, for our murderous assumption revelation might
    end.

Forgive our staunch disbelief in the world we see,
our assuming an Earth unseeded by the sacred, our shying
from the firmament that stirs beneath our feet. Forgive us
for placing such stringent gates on compassion, for
    defaulting
from our native communion with our kind, for not
    remembering
the fellowness in the eyes of feral creatures.

Forgive us our failure to meet your countenance
within the glistening body of this world.

Have mercy on us who have neglected your inscription
on the pages of our days and dismissed the disciplined
magic that would see you reborn. Have mercy on us all
who have committed uncountable sins against beauty
and declined our roles in the chorus of creation.

III

The heavens and the earth and the surging sea:
these are the testaments to your tenacity and craft,
the marvels that prompt human mouths to praise.
The heavens, wheeling with your lights and swept by your
    breath,
are laced with our moisture, contaminates, speed,
our prodigal spending of Earth's darkened blood.
The seas are alive with your dwindling splendour,
the unknowable addition of our heat and our filth,
the trawling of abundance to an underworld of shades.
The earth is charged with a great and diminishing grandeur,
a contraction of the fabulous lexicon of animals,
its abundance pocked by the marks of our pillage.

May the delicately painted winged carriers of God,
the flickering and flippered lithe swimmers of God,
the wolves and the howling gangs of God –
may you whose immense range of shape and sensation
so vastly surpasses and excites our own:
may you have mercy on us who have cast you to poverty,
who have failed to shepherd your most precious works.

We are a species cherished sorely in your affection,
a brief poem glinting in one galaxy's life. We are
a feast of blunders, bile, and desecration – and we are the
    flowering
where you face in surprise and delight
what your own unseen fingers and ours have formed.
We wish you the pleasures of unending invention, the
    planting
by fractions of your mind in flesh. We wish you

96

the flourishing of your exuberant arts – from winking cell
to the complex cathedral of the cortex. We wish you
the fondness and fertility of your ravishing works,
the articulate expansion of all the eloquence you are.

IV

I believe in the patient gestations that give birth
to the Earth: in attraction's gravity, chemistry's
charms, in the squirrelling and sprouting lush genesis of life,
the perpetual revision of flesh and idea. I believe
in one God and in many gods, in all the maculate
immaculate conceptions of the sacred, in all things invisible
in this visible world. I believe in the embracing
multi-limbed Beloved, in the kneeling and wantonness
it elicits in our hearts, in one who beggars
all my knowledge of who they are. I believe
in each god who has stretched the spirit of a creature
and shattered a brittle recalcitrance of thought;
who has moulded a human mouth to awe
and rivered its fire into vivid blood. I believe
in all the extravagant lineages of grace,
in the breeding of creeds to what surpasses each one,
in religion's still unfinished tapestries of joy.

And I believe in living in the great *as if,*
in walking in the slippers and myths of the dead,
in tracking the tales that balance this world on the web
of their fingers. I believe in the herd and host
of incipient spirits who unfurl within the volumes
of story and verse, in the cataracts of wonder
that human artistry unlocks. I believe in the keen

and manifold body, in the delights of living in this palace
of flesh, in the brilliance and crystal of our senses'
wide windows. I believe in the munificent beauty
that pours itself through our momentary lives,
in the profuse and imaginary wealth of this world.

I believe in a universe elaborate with listening, in a bounty
who craves the patterned solace of call and response,
the limitless circuit of attending speech. I believe beneath all
in the one who seeks itself in a myriad of voices, its lips
always parting in exaltations of song.

V

Blessed are those from each site on this manging globe
who come in the name of revering what is here.
Blessed are those pledged to the holiness of each biota,
who tell the religious history of the spheres, unravelling
the awe in electron, flesh, and art. Blessed are those
who've been called and converted by beauty,
who seek forms with the force to restore this world.

May we recall you from pole to melting pole,
in each vestige of your plumage gracing this planet.
May we attend the wisdom into which we were given birth
and the scriptures penned in parallel with our years on this
    planet.
May we find and invoke your names in time
and be gathered toward a peace that may yet be yours.

May this generation, bequeathed with a richness we have
    barely

begun to perceive – may we know our clear
powers wedded to the wishes of this world. Enrol us
again in a colloquy with a universe who speaks,
that we might not succumb to the depletion of this world,
to the atrophy of all our faculties of wonder. Call us
to imagine a religion equal to our era's labours, a maker
or a making to sustain us through this gasp in time.

May we be animate with the instincts and instilling
of listening and song. May we lend our voices
to the muted Earth and serve as the cantors
of its common life, that creation's sweet lyric
might sing out the reaches of each of its names.

Notes

"Eyes Turn Blue": Qur'an 53.43-7, 52.22-4, 76.15-21,
    20.100-102

"Conversion": I Corinthians 15.8-9, Acts 9.1-9

"Paul, Apostate": Romans 16.25, I Corinthians 2.7,
    Galatians 6.17, Colossians 1.15, 2.9

"A New Husband": Romans 7.1-6

"I Know a Man": II Corinthians 12.1-5

"Megha": The story of Megha is told in *Buddhist
    Scriptures*, selected and translated by Edward Conze

"Veil of Flesh": Hebrews 10.19-20

"Prince of the Universe": "Prince and master of the
    universe" is one of the names of Muhammad

"Jacob, Wrestling": Genesis 32.22-32

"Law of the Flesh": Romans 7.14-25

"Tonguing the Mouths": I Corinthians 13

"Pursuing our Pleasure in the Body of Christ": I
    Corinthians 12.12-27, Romans 12.4-5

"A Wish to Be Mary": Luke 1. 26-38

"Krishna in the Desert": The story is told in *The
    Adventures of Young Krishna* by Diksha Dalal- Clayton

"Saul at Ramah": I Samuel 19.18-24

"Captives": Michelangelo's sculptures at the Louvre

"Two Boys on a Riverbank": Claude Monet's "Jean-Pierre
    Hoschedé and Michel Monet on the Banks of the
    Epte," in the collection of the National Gallery of
    Canada in Ottawa

"Hunters": Acts 10.9-16; the story of Krishna is told in *Ka*
    by Roberto Calasso
"Mating Our Faiths": Romans 11.16-24, Ephesians 2.14-
    16
"Imageless Image": Colossians 1.15, I Corinthians 15.28
"Sea of Ink": Qur'an 18.109, 31.27
"Continuing the Story": Philippians 2.12-13, Colossians
    1.24
"Driven to the Wilderness": Mark 1.12-13
"All in All": Romans 8.18-22, I Corinthians 15.28
"Magnificat": Luke 1. 46-55, 67-79
"Anointing": Luke 4.18-19
"Continuing the Party": John 2.1-11

Acknowledgements

This book was produced with the support of the Ontario Arts Council. "The Bears' House" first appeared in *Descant*. "Luke" and "Below me in Blue" first appeared in *The Antigonish Review*. Thanks to Janet McClelland and Bryan Young.

About Brian Day's Previous Collections

A vibrantly alive Jesus, complete with homoerotic desires, emerges from the poetry of Brian Day in his new book *Conjuring Jesus* ... His poems can stand alone as works of art. – Kittredge Cherry in *Lambda Literary*

There is a sustained spiritual attention in Brian Day's *Azure* – with mostly Eastern but also biblical elements – combined with a luxurious sensuality manifest in almost every poem. – *The University of Toronto Quarterly*

Brian Day's *Love Is Not Native to My Blood* is an extraordinarily accomplished first volume, in its cultural breadth and its verbal richness ... At home in both traditional rhymed stanzas and freer forms, Day writes a language that is solid and tactile. – *The University of Toronto Quarterly*